C000193356

Jesus
The wounded Saviour

6 GROUP BIBLE STUDIES FOR LENT

Selwyn Hughes
with Ian Sewter

Contents

Introduction

As we approach Easter we embark on a theme which I trust will not only deepen your love for the Lord Jesus Christ, but will help you understand in an even greater way the truth of His ability to enter into and sympathise with every phase of human need. Let it be said at once – our Lord is a wounded healer. That is to say, His ability to heal our wounds flows from the fact that He Himself has experienced our wounds. The God we see in Jesus has been in our condition. He has gone through everything we have to go through. His wounds answer our wounds.

Throughout time, humans, in manufacturing their gods out of their imaginations, made them appear victorious and strong, aloof from the hurts and sorrows of life on earth. They thought that to show them as being affected by the problems of humanity would make them appear weak and inadequate, and betray their earthliness. Their strength (so they believed) lay in their aloofness. They had to be always strong, always victorious. But how different is the truth about the real God! As Edward Shillito puts it in his poem 'Jesus of the Scars':

> The other gods were strong, but Thou wast weak;
> They rode, but Thou didst stumble to a throne;
> But to our wounds only God's wounds can speak,
> And not a god has wounds, but Thou alone.

No other god can speak to my condition because no other god has been in my condition. Nothing can be more wonderful in earth and heaven than to know that when we come to Jesus, we come to One who has worn our flesh, measured its frailty and knows exactly how we feel. The willingness of our Creator to subject Himself to the conditions under which we live must surely spell out one thing – God is intensely interested in the hurts and sorrows that attend the human condition. He did not pick us up with a pair of celestial tongs and hold us before His gaze in order to study and understand our sufferings – He wrapped Himself in our flesh and experienced our pains in the same way we experience them. And His interest flows, not to *some* of His creation but to *all* His creation.

You may be familiar with the famous painting by Charles E. Butler which is entitled *The King of Kings*. It is a fine and beautiful painting which depicts Jesus Christ standing at the foot of His cross and receiving the homage of the crowned heads of the world. In the background is the defeated Prince of Darkness who watches as the monarchs of the world press in to do Christ honour. Altogether 158 portraits are included, and only two are not royal personages – George Washington and Oliver Cromwell. The intention of the painter to depict Christ as the King of kings is to be commended, but some have criticised it on the grounds that it implies Christ is interested only in the noble and great. That was not Butler's intention, of course, but I can see how some might draw that conclusion. The truth is that the eye of Jesus is held, not by the crown on a person's head, but by the ache in their heart. When He was here on earth, He had a special concern for those whom life had wounded. And what He was He is, and what He is He was, and what He is and was He ever will be.

A question which is often asked by those passing through deep emotional trauma is: how can Christ enter into my feelings when He did not experience the same kind of situation I am going through at present? A man once said to me, when I tried to offer him the comfort of Christ at the death of his three-month-old baby, 'Jesus didn't know what it was to lose a child, for He was never a father. How can He really understand what my wife and I are feeling at this moment?' The answer I gave him was this: although the problems we face in our world are varied and different, those problems produce a pain in our heart that is shared in the same way by everyone. I asked, 'How would you describe the pain you are feeling in your heart at this moment?' Without hesitation he replied, 'Desolating grief and sorrow.' I pointed out to him that although Christ had not passed through the identical circumstances through which he and his wife had just passed, He most certainly had felt, and felt equally keenly, the pain of 'desolating grief' which was going on in his heart. That truth appeared to comfort him as it has comforted many others with whom I have shared it. I hope it might also comfort you. The problems on the surface of our lives may have different wrappings, but deep down in our hearts the pain we experience has the same labels – hurt, sadness, grief, emptiness, despair, disappointment. The problems in our world lead to pain in the heart and it is that pain, whatever its label, that Christ has touched somewhere on the journey between His birth and His death. No wonder our Lord is referred to by so many as 'the comforting Christ'.

No matter how positive and optimistic our outlook may be, we must never deny what we are feeling at the moment. We need not be dragged down by our feelings into a whirlpool of despair, but we must be willing to face and feel those emotions. That is the principle of mental and emotional health which Jesus knew, understood and practised. So, standing by the tomb of Lazarus, He allows His grief to find expression. The tears start from His eyes. He really feels, does this man of Galilee. Remember, when next you experience suffering or wounds of any kind that He who wept at the grave of His dearest friend not only knows how you feel, but will impart to you His unfailing strength and power. Praise His wonderful name!

Suggestions for using this book

Each study should take between one and one-and-a-half hours. Groups work best when all members participate and therefore perhaps different people could read or lead each section (which may require a little advance preparation). Whoever is leading the group should try to involve everyone, especially those who like to think more deeply before contributing. Sometimes a simple 'George (or Geraldine), what do you think?' is sufficient to unlock pearls of wisdom and inspiration from someone who has not yet spoken. At the end of each study there could be a time of open prayer. Above all, remember that this is not meant to be extensive preparation for an examination but enjoyable preparation for life and a time of fellowship where disciples of Jesus come together to encourage one another and discover more about Him.

Humiliation and Loneliness

Icebreaker

Describe a time when you have been embarrassed or lonely. What feelings did you experience?

Opening Prayer

Dear Father, as we start our Lent study looking at the way Jesus was wounded so that we might be comforted and healed, please help us understand Your Word and Your heart. We thank You for Your Holy Spirit and ask that He may give us insights beyond our natural abilities. Help us, Lord, to be open to each other and to You as we share in this study of Your Word together. We pray that those of us who are naturally extrovert will be sensitive to those who are not, and that You would give those who are more reserved, unusual boldness to share their special insights, so that we may all benefit. We ask not that we would simply gain more knowledge, but that we might grow in faith, and experience more of Your presence and power in our lives. In Jesus' name. Amen.

Bible Readings

Philippians 2:3–11

Do nothing out of selfish ambition or vain conceit, but in humility consider others better than yourselves. Each of you should look not only to your own interests, but also to the interests of others. Your attitude should be the same as that of Christ Jesus: Who, being in very nature God, did not consider equality with God something to be grasped, but made himself nothing, taking the very nature of a servant, being made in human likeness. And being found in appearance as a man, he humbled himself and became obedient to death – even death on a cross! Therefore God exalted him to the highest place and gave him the name that is above every name, that at the name of Jesus every knee should bow, in heaven and on earth and under the earth, and every tongue confess that Jesus Christ is Lord, to the glory of God the Father.

Mark 14:50, 15:25–34

… everyone deserted him and fled. … It was the third hour when they crucified him. The written notice of the charge against him read: THE KING OF THE JEWS. They crucified two robbers with him, one on his right and one on his left. Those who passed by hurled insults at him, shaking their heads and saying, 'So! You who are going to destroy the temple and build it in three days, come down from the cross and save yourself!' In the same way the chief priests and the teachers of the law mocked him among themselves. 'He saved others,' they said, 'but he can't save himself! Let this Christ, this King of Israel, come down now from the cross, that we may see and believe.' Those crucified with him also heaped insults on him. At the sixth hour darkness came over the whole land until the ninth hour. And at the ninth hour Jesus cried out in a loud voice, '*Eloi, Eloi, lama sabachthani?*' – which means, 'My God, my God, why have you forsaken me?'

Setting the Scene

The picture of the true God presented to us in the Scriptures is that of the Creator of the universe who took upon Himself the form of a servant and was made in the likeness of men. Only the strong can dare to become weak, and so strong was our Creator that He subjected Himself to the most astonishing humiliation and became a human being – just like us. Charles Spurgeon, the great preacher of a bygone age, put it like this: 'For God to become a man was more humiliation than for an angel to become a worm.'

Why did He do it? There are many reasons, but listen to what the great writer Dorothy Sayers has to say about it:

> For whatever reason God chose to make man as he is
> – limited and suffering and subject to sorrows and death –
> He had the honesty and courage to take His own medicine.
> Whatever game He is playing with His creation, He has
> kept His own rules and played fair. He can exact nothing
> from man that He has not exacted of Himself. He Himself
> has gone through the whole of human experience; from the
> trivial irritations of family life and the cramping restrictions
> of hard work to the worst horrors of pain and humiliation.

Because God came and put Himself in our condition,
He now fully understands our condition. How amazing!
I don't know about you, but a God who gave Himself to
me in this way is a God who can have my heart any day.

Opening our Eyes

I think Jesus knew a deep sense of loneliness as no one
knew it before or since. As a child, He must have felt a
little apart – not superior (though He was superior), but
a sense of being different. At the age of twelve He knew
that He must be about His Father's business. When His
ministry began, it caused concern among some of the
members of His family. Other men have known what it
is like to have all the world take up arms against them,
but usually they had someone at home who would take
up arms beside them against the world. Jesus lacked
even that. The other children born to Mary and Joseph
and who formed part of Christ's earthly family came to
believe that He did not know what He was doing and
were astonished by His actions (Mark 3:20–21). In what
remained of His earthly life, it was to His disciples He
looked for understanding and companionship – but
He looked in vain. On the eve of His crucifixion they

argued about precedence, they slept while He agonised in the Garden, and they ran away at the moment He was arrested. Many of the world's martyrs knew at the moment of their death that there were some in the world who sympathised with them and understood the cause for which they died. But Jesus had little sympathy and little understanding. His sacrifice mystified the people who were closest to Him. As Dr Sangster, the famous Methodist preacher, put it: 'It mattered to all the world that He died for love, but no single soul in the world understood that He was doing it. He was lonely with the awful loneliness of God.' How can it be doubted that He is able to sympathise with anyone who is engulfed by loneliness?

Consider also the 'cry of dereliction'. The phrase is used by theologians to describe the feelings of abandonment which our Lord appeared to experience when He cried out from the cross, 'My God, my God, why have you forsaken me?' Throughout the history of the Church, great debates have taken place on this matter of our Lord's 'cry of dereliction'. Some believe He was not actually abandoned by God but felt abandoned, while others take the view that it was much more than a feeling and that on the cross He actually was forsaken by God. I find myself in agreement with the latter of these two beliefs. R.W. Dale, in his book *The Atonement*,[1] convinced me of this when he wrote: 'I decline to accept any explanation of these words which implies that they do not represent the actual truth of our Lord's position. I cannot believe that Jesus was uttering a false cry.' Just imagine it – our Lord, who had been forsaken by men, was now being forsaken by God. As He began to experience in His soul the suffering of sin (not His own sin, but ours) and proceeded through His sufferings to pay the terrifying debt that sin had built up in the universe, God, who could have nothing to do with sin, had to turn His back upon Him. Our Lord plunged into the darkness of sin and endured the awful suffering of the atonement entirely

on His own. Jesus experienced on the cross not just a felt, but a real abandonment – something those who are Christians will never experience. Let this solemn but glorious truth take hold of you today – because He was abandoned, you will never be abandoned (Heb. 13:5b).

Discussion Starters

1. In what ways did Jesus experience humiliation?

2. Describe Christ's attitude to His humiliation.

3. In what ways did Jesus experience loneliness?

4. How might feelings of humiliation and loneliness have a long-term effect upon us?

5. What do you think about Christ's 'cry of dereliction'?

_____

_____

_____

_____

6. Why is it possible to never give in to feelings of abandonment?

_____

_____

_____

_____

7. In what sense is Christ a wounded healer?

_____

_____

_____

_____

8. Is it possible for a Christian never to feel lonely?

_____

_____

_____

_____

Final Thoughts

Some forms of loneliness may remain part of our human condition until we die and go to heaven. Is this watering down the effectiveness of the Holy Spirit or the joy which Christ gives to us? I believe not. No one is more confident of the power of Christ to work miracles and overcome problems than I, but there are some issues that will never be fully resolved until we get to heaven – and loneliness may be one of them. Some might never struggle with loneliness, for they will be surrounded with love and affection until the day they die, but others will not be so blessed. What about such people? They can either pretend they are not lonely and refuse to grapple honestly with their condition, or accept the fact that they may continue through life with a groan in their heart, a groan that is relieved by the presence of Christ but not always eliminated. A friend of mine who is a counsellor tells his counsellees, 'It's OK to hurt.' He says that sometimes they appear relieved that they are given permission to feel that way. Some hurts are part of the human condition and they may be with us until the day we die, but remember this – Christ's presence can be there to relieve and support so that the pain is not incapacitating. We are not absolutely sure what Paul's 'thorn in the flesh' was, but the important thing to remember is that while God did not deliver him from it, He was certainly there with him in it. God always gives enough grace to carry on (2 Cor. 12:7–10).

Closing Prayer

Lord Jesus, we thank You that You became human and suffered humiliation and loneliness just like us. You do not simply offer us heavenly wisdom, but the sympathy and understanding that come from earthly experience. You are truly a wonderful Saviour. Amen.

NOTE

1. R.W. Dale, *The Atonement* (Congregation Union of England and Wales, London, 1909); this book is still available from Quinta Press, Shropshire, England: see quintapress@mac.com.

Temptation

Icebreaker

Describe the thoughts that go through people's minds when they have committed themselves to diet and are then confronted by one of their favourite cream buns.

What would you think if you were driving along a clear motorway to the airport early in the morning to catch a plane and you were behind schedule?

Opening Prayer

Father, You know the temptations we face in our lives. We thank You that there is forgiveness when we fail and give in to them. But we pray, Lord, that through this session we will learn, like Jesus, to overcome temptations through Your Word and Your power. Rather than seek Your mercy after we have sinned we seek Your grace to walk in righteousness. Help us to understand and live in the balance of Your resources and our personal responsibility. Father, help us not to welcome sin but to reject it even as You do. In Jesus' name. Amen.

Bible Readings

Matthew 4:1–11

Then Jesus was led by the Spirit into the desert to be tempted by the devil. After fasting for forty days and forty nights, he was hungry. The tempter came to him and said, 'If you are the Son of God, tell these stones to become bread.'

Jesus answered, 'It is written: "Man does not live on bread alone, but on every word that comes from the mouth of God."'

Then the devil took him to the holy city and had him stand on the highest point of the temple. 'If you are the

Son of God,' he said, 'throw yourself down. For it is written: "He will command his angels concerning you, and they will lift you up in their hands, so that you will not strike your foot against a stone."'

Jesus answered him, 'It is also written: "Do not put the Lord your God to the test."'

Again, the devil took him to a very high mountain and showed him all the kingdoms of the world and their splendour. 'All this I will give you,' he said, 'if you will bow down and worship me.'

Jesus said to him, 'Away from me, Satan! For it is written: "Worship the Lord your God, and serve him only."' Then the devil left him, and angels came and attended him.

James 1:12–15; 4:7

Blessed is the man who perseveres under trial, because when he has stood the test, he will receive the crown of life that God has promised to those who love him. When tempted, no-one should say, 'God is tempting me.' For God cannot be tempted by evil, nor does he tempt anyone; but each one is tempted when, by his own evil desire, he is dragged away and enticed. Then, after desire has conceived, it gives birth to sin; and sin, when it is full-grown, gives birth to death. … Submit yourselves, then, to God. Resist the devil, and he will flee from you.

Setting the Scene

Before we focus on Christ's temptations, let's consider the subject of temptation in general. Why is temptation so 'successful'? What makes it work? How can we handle it? These are questions that constantly appear in my correspondence. Mark Antony, you may remember, was known as 'the silver-throated orator of Rome'. He was a brilliant statesman and magnificent in battle. He had, however, the fatal flaw of moral weakness, and one day

his tutor confronted him with these words: 'O Marcus
… able to conquer the world, but unable to resist a
temptation.' That indictment, I'm afraid, applies not just to
Mark Antony but to almost everyone. When I was young,
a close Christian friend of mine used to say, facetiously, 'I
can resist anything but temptation.'

It is important, I believe, to differentiate between a trial
and a temptation. Generally speaking, a trial is an ordeal
or a test of our faith, while a temptation is a deliberate
enticement to do evil. God cannot tempt us, but He can
and does allow tests to try us. Normally there is nothing
immoral involved in experiencing a trial. It is a hardship,
an ordeal, but not an enticement to evil. Temptation
involves a definite enticement to do wrong. The
dictionary says: 'To tempt someone is to beguile them to
do wrong, by promise of pleasure or gain.' Temptation
motivates a person to be bad by promising something that
appears to be good. Isn't that just like the devil?

Opening our Eyes

Today we ask ourselves: did our Lord know what it
was to be tempted? Was our Lord put through the same
pressures that we go through when we are tempted to go
another way than God's? No one has ever experienced
such a depth and a degree of temptation as did Jesus.
One argument goes: how can Christ understand our
feelings unless He knew what it was to experience all our
feelings? In answering that question, I must remind you
about Christ meeting us, not at the surface of life where
there are so many differences, but in the depths where
we are all the same. Underneath all temptations the
basic issue is this – an enticement to act independently
of God. Hold that in your mind and you will not go
wrong in understanding Christ's involvement with our
human nature. Did He experience the temptation to take

an easier road – to act independently of God? I have no doubt myself that the three temptations levelled at Christ in that rigorous and severe encounter in the wilderness were the most powerful temptations a human being has ever experienced on this earth. But our Lord showed that obedience to God is possible even in the most difficult of situations. The first Adam failed in a garden feasting, but the second Adam triumphed in a wilderness fasting. Can Jesus succour those who are passing through the fires of temptation? I know of no one better – do you?

How do we resist temptation? The biblical answer is so simple that many stumble over it. It is found in Galatians 5:23 and the word I want to focus on is self-control. The Greek word literally means 'in strength', and that's exactly what happens when the Holy Spirit resides in us – He comes in to strengthen us on the inside. In other words, God promises that through His Spirit, we will be able to master our turbulent feelings in the moment of temptation. Pause and let that sink in. Now some may be saying at this stage, 'Wait a minute – dealing with temptation is not something I have to do, but something God does for me. I am not able to do anything about temptation and unless He does it in and through me, I am sunk. God is the active one and I am the passive one.' Now there is a grain of truth in this, for it is true that the more we allow God to work in and through us by His Holy Spirit, the more power we have at our disposal, but ultimately we have to put it to work though deliberate choice and conscious action. It is like engaging the clutch in a manually-controlled car. The engine may be running at a very fast rate, but there will be no forward or backward movement of the car until the driver makes a conscious decision to avail himself of the power of the engine by engaging the clutch.

Whatever view we might hold about the work of the Holy Spirit in our life, the bottom line is this – God holds us

responsible for shouting a thunderous 'No!' to sin. I am to decide, whenever I am faced with the possibility of yielding to sin, that I will not do so because I reject sin even as God does. Victory depends upon believing and accepting the fact that God's power is sufficient to resist the seemingly overwhelming rush of internal feelings and urges, and deciding not to yield. If you try to deal passively with temptation and turn the responsibility over to God, then you will fail. Self-control comes from God, but we have to carry it out. He supplies the power – we supply the willingness. Note that this is not so much the self being in control which implies mere human effort, but the Holy Spirit helping our spirits to control our selves – our minds, our emotions and our bodies.

Above all, remember the life of Christ, our wounded Healer. Scripture says of Him, 'Because he himself suffered when he was tempted, he is able to help those who are being tempted' and 'For we do not have a high priest who is unable to sympathise with our weaknesses, but we have one who has been tempted in every way, just as we are – yet was without sin' (Heb. 2:18; 4:15).

Discussion Starters

1. Can you agree on a definition of temptation?

_____

_____

_____

_____

2. Can you agree on an outline of the process of temptation?

_____

_____

_____

_____

3. What makes temptation so difficult to resist?

_____

_____

_____

_____

4. What is the goal of all temptation?

_____

_____

_____

_____

5. How can we successfully resist temptation?

_____

_____

_____

_____

6. How did Christ overcome temptations?

_____

_____

_____

_____

7. Compare the natural inclinations of a Christian and someone who does not know Christ.

_____

_____

_____

_____

8. What temptations do you face that you would like others to pray about?

_____

_____

_____

_____

Final Thoughts

Some years ago, when talking to a Christian man who told me he had homosexual inclinations and found himself at times yielding to those desires, I was not surprised to find that his view of temptation ran something like this: 'Whenever I have been tempted, I try to "let go and let God" as I have been taught, but my urges always seem to carry me to my homosexual partner.' (Let me make it clear that despite the woolly thinking in some parts of the Christian Church, I regard homosexual practice as sin.) Further conversation revealed that he was looking for victory from two sources: either that the desire would be weakened, or that greater strength would be given to him by God to resist the desire. Notice, neither option depended on him at all. He was responsible for nothing. He was passively saying, 'Lord, I don't really want to sin; help me.' I pointed out that his responsibility was to decide assertively not to sin, and then trust God to work in him both to will and to act according to His good pleasure. The strength to resist was there in his life in great abundance (as it is also in yours if you are a Christian), but victory depended on his assuming responsibility for what he could control – making a clear and clean-cut decision to obey God by not sinning. The same basic supply of the Spirit is given to every child of God, but it is our responsibility to carry out the action of self-control before victory can be seen in our lives.

Closing Prayer

Our Father in heaven, hallowed be Your name, Your kingdom come, Your will be done on earth as it is in heaven. Give us today our daily bread. Forgive us our trespasses, as we forgive those who trespass against us. And lead us not into temptation, but deliver us from evil. For Thine is the kingdom, the power and the glory. For ever and ever. Amen.

Misunderstanding and Bereavement

Icebreaker

My cousin once spent fifteen minutes shouting and banging on our fence trying to wake my father, apparently asleep in the garden. The figure he saw on a bench through a hole in the gate was actually a Guy Fawkes made for Bonfire Night dressed in my father's old clothes! What misunderstandings have you experienced that have been humorous, and which have been painful?

Opening Prayer

Dear Father, we thank You that Your peace passes all understanding and also passes all misunderstanding. As we consider the pain caused by misunderstanding and bereavement, Lord, please help us to be sensitive to one another; walk with us to comfort us through valleys of shadows, so that we experience the clarity of Your wisdom and love. Amen.

Bible Readings

John 1:1–11

In the beginning was the Word, and the Word was with God, and the Word was God. He was with God in the beginning.

Through him all things were made; without him nothing was made that has been made. In him was life, and that life was the light of men. The light shines in the darkness, but the darkness has not understood it.

There came a man who was sent from God; his name was John. He came as a witness to testify concerning that light, so that through him all men might believe. He himself was not the light; he came only as a witness to the light. The true light that gives light to every man was coming into the world.

He was in the world, and though the world was made

through him, the world did not recognise him. He came to that which was his own, but his own did not receive him.

John 11:32–38

When Mary reached the place where Jesus was and saw him, she fell at his feet and said, 'Lord, if you had been here, my brother would not have died.'

When Jesus saw her weeping, and the Jews who had come along with her also weeping, he was deeply moved in spirit and troubled. 'Where have you laid him?' he asked.

'Come and see, Lord,' they replied.

Jesus wept.

Then the Jews said, 'See how he loved him!'

But some of them said, 'Could not he who opened the eyes of the blind man have kept this man from dying?'

Jesus, once more deeply moved, came to the tomb. It was a cave with a stone laid across the entrance.

Setting the Scene

Another earthly circumstance which our Lord was called to pass through was that of being misunderstood. Few things are more difficult to live with than being misunderstood. Sometimes it's downright unbearable. One author calls it 'the paralysing sting of humanity'. When I first read that description of 'misunderstanding', I felt the writer was overstating the issue, but the more I have thought about the feelings that are generated through misunderstanding, the more I have come to agree. When you are misunderstood, you have no defence. Perhaps you have been in such a situation recently – or you may be passing through such a phase at this very moment. Have you noticed when you are misunderstood, no matter how hard you try to correct the misunderstanding, it doesn't seem to get you anywhere? Usually, it gets worse. You get all your facts lined up, ready to make things clear, and all you get are blank

looks of incredulity and unbelief. The harder you work to make your motives clear, the worse it gets and the deeper it hurts. Yes, the sting of being misunderstood can be truly 'paralysing'. I don't think there is a person alive who has not at some time or another felt misunderstood. When analysed, misunderstanding can be seen as having two elements: one, an innocent remark or statement that is misinterpreted, and two, the offence that arises in the heart of another due to the mistaken interpretation. Jesus was constantly being misunderstood. Every statement and utterance that fell from His lips came from a heart of love, but still He was misinterpreted and thus maligned. Our Lord was also touched with grief over the loss of a loved one when He was here on earth. I am thinking particularly of Christ's sorrow over the deaths of His relative and prophetic forerunner, John the Baptist, and also His close friend Lazarus. Believe me, no one knows better than our Lord what it means to be misunderstood and to experience bereavement.

Opening our Eyes

Misunderstanding often arises from an innocent word or implication. Nothing was meant by it, but it was misread and an offence created. Apart from Christ, one of the most misunderstood men in Scripture was King David, and a brief examination of his life and circumstances will illustrate for us the dynamics of misunderstanding. When David was anointed with oil by Samuel, the statement was effectively made to Jesse's family: 'Your youngest is going to be king.' But learning how to be king included learning how to endure being misunderstood. Saul, the current king of Israel, had deep problems in his life which became apparent soon after he had been appointed. He was a deeply insecure person and, like all insecure people, tried to compensate for his failings by such things as people-pleasing, attention-getting and so on. One day, when returning from a battle with the Philistines in company with David, he heard the women singing a song they had composed in honour of the victory: 'Saul has slain his thousands, and David his tens of thousands' (1 Sam. 18:7). Saul was deeply upset. It was not just the 9,000 difference that bothered him, but the fact that David was getting the glory. Notice what he said: 'What more can he get but the kingdom?' But David was not after the kingdom. He was Saul's man, and amongst other things his personal musician. The innocent acts of David were so misinterpreted by Saul that thereafter David's life became almost unbearable. If it's any comfort, being misunderstood has always been the standard operating procedure for those whom God appoints to special service. You do not grow fully or completely without being misunderstood. So learn to bring all your misunderstandings to Him. Early in my ministry I was involved in a situation where I was so misunderstood that I thought the pain would never go away. Crushed and bruised, all I could do was wait. The memory of the event is still there, but the sting has gone and something very beautiful has come out of it. I would not give a penny for the pain, but I would not take a million pounds for what has emerged in my life because of it.

Generally speaking, loss falls into two categories – loss of people, and loss of things such as the loss of a job or the loss of personal necessities and benefits. The natural reaction to deep loss is that of grief, and any attempt to avoid this can lead to all kinds of spiritual and psychological problems. So don't try to escape grief by any illusions or subterfuges, for the illusions and subterfuges will in the end turn out to be worse than the grief itself. Some Christians teach that the way to deal with all the troublesome issues of life (even the loss of a loved one) is to lift your heart to God in thanksgiving and focus only on Him. If you dwell on the negatives, they say, you will allow the seeds of doubt to invade

your heart and this will undermine your spiritual life and bring you into bondage to doubt and unbelief. All error is truth out of balance, and this error, like so many others, has a kernel of truth – but it is not truth in balance. It is true that when calamity strikes, we should focus on God, but it is not true that we should seek to escape from the feelings of loss and grief that are the natural reaction of the soul. Notice how those who shared the experience with Job said nothing, but simply sat in silence (Job 2:13). Jesus allowed Himself to feel grief, and feel it so fully that He was deeply moved and cried real tears at the tomb of Lazarus. Consider also Christ's response when told of the death of John the Baptist: 'When Jesus heard what had happened, he withdrew by boat privately to a solitary place' (Matt.14:13). Jesus, when here on earth, really felt grief. Remember, when next you grieve, that He who wept at the grave of His dearest friend not only knows how you feel, but will impart to you His unfailing strength and power.

Discussion Starters

1. Why may others misunderstand us?

_____

_____

_____

2. Do you agree or disagree that being misunderstood is like a 'paralysing sting'?

_____

_____

_____

3. How should we respond when we are misunderstood?

_____

_____

_____

4. Why can being misunderstood be good for us?

_____

_____

_____

5. Why has God designed us in such a way that we experience grief?

_____

_____

_____

6. Why should we allow ourselves to feel grief and not suppress it?

_____

_____

_____

7. How should we minister to people experiencing grief?

_____

_____

_____

8. How did Jesus experience misunderstanding and grief, and what does that mean for us?

_____

_____

_____

Final Thoughts

Probably no one in the history of the world was more misunderstood than Jesus Christ. He came to earth offering love, pouring it out passionately and prodigally on all who were in need, but the more He ministered, the more He was misunderstood. The people among whom He had been brought up misunderstood Him. His own immediate family misunderstood Him. Even His disciples, who spent so much time in His presence and knew Him more closely than any others – they, too, misunderstood Him. When it comes to the issue of being misunderstood or not being understood (there is a slight difference between the two), remember that no one has touched this as deeply as Jesus. Take comfort in the thought that when other helpers fail and comforts flee – there is always Jesus.

Joe Bayly, a Christian writer who lost three of his teenage children, says in his book *The View from a Hearse*: 'One of the best contributions we can make to a person going through intense suffering and loss is our presence without words, not even verses of Scripture dumped into the ears of the grieving.'[1] An individual reeling from the blow of a calamity like the loss of a loved one usually has a broken heart. The soil of the soul is not yet ready for the implanting of the heavenly seed. It will be ready later, but not right away. Never forget that, for many a soul has been damaged by well-meaning Christians who said the right thing, but at the wrong time. When Jesus met the two on the way to Emmaus who were so obviously overcome by grief, He did not immediately expound the Scriptures to them, but walked alongside them for a while, asking gentle questions, until He knew that they were ready for what He wanted to share with them. It is many years since the death of my wife, and I think I can now look back upon the event with a little more objectivity than before. The people who most helped and encouraged me in those early days when grief was tearing at my soul, were not those who told me that God would use this to deepen my ministry and greatly extend my influence and service for Him (though that was certainly true), but those who simply said, 'We know you are hurting, and for what it is worth we want you to know – we hurt for you too.' The first thing a person who is grieving needs to know is not that something good will come out of the experience, but that someone cares. Our Lord, the wounded Healer, truly cares.

Closing Prayer

Dear Lord Jesus, once again we are amazed to recognise how deeply You were wounded when You lived amongst us. We thank You that because You were wounded by misunderstanding and bereavement You do not just offer the comfort of words but the comfort of experience. Help us to be honest with our own feelings, and honest with You. Amen.

NOTE

1. Joseph Bayly, *The View from a Hearse: a Christian View of Death* (Elgin, Il., USA: David C. Cook, 1969).

Criticism and Prejudice

Icebreaker

Do you agree with the well-known saying, 'Sticks and stones may break my bones but words will never hurt me'? Can you give examples from your own life to support your view?

Opening Prayer

Dear Father, we come before You not simply to know more of Your Word but to know more of Your Son and to experience His transforming power in our lives. Help us to be among those whose words bring help not hindrance, comfort not sorrow, healing not wounds, and life not death. Amen.

Bible Readings

1 Peter 2:21–23

To this you were called, because Christ suffered for you, leaving you an example, that you should follow in his steps. 'He committed no sin, and no deceit was found in his mouth.' When they hurled their insults at him, he did not retaliate; when he suffered, he made no threats. Instead, he entrusted himself to him who judges justly.

Ephesians 4:29–32

Do not let any unwholesome talk come out of your mouths, but only what is helpful for building others up according to their needs, that it may benefit those who listen. And do not grieve the Holy Spirit of God, with whom you were sealed for the day of redemption. Get rid of all bitterness, rage and anger, brawling and slander, along with every form of malice. Be kind and compassionate to one another, forgiving each other, just as in Christ God forgave you.

Setting the Scene

Another set of experiences which Christ faced, is that of coping with cruel and unjust criticism. When I first began to write *Every Day with Jesus* forty years ago, I used to receive many letters of criticism, most of which, I have to say, were helpful and constructive. Some, however, were devastatingly negative and hurt me deeply. Over the years, as I have learned to express myself more clearly and have taken pains to make plain my meaning, the destructively critical letters have dwindled and become just a trickle. As I write this, however, I have had several letters of criticism: one constructive, the others destructive. I am trying to analyse my reactions as I write these lines, and I have to admit that the ones that are destructive and which are clearly based on spite have the effect of producing within me feelings of deep hurt. I know that I must accept some responsibility for my hurt feelings because I am a rational being, and my feelings follow my thoughts and the meaning I give to an event. By that I mean the way I evaluate a situation determines my feelings, not necessarily the event itself – hence I have a responsibility to evaluate things correctly and put them in their right perspective. Allowing for all that, however, I still feel hurt.

The issue of bigotry and prejudice was something else our Lord experienced, for He was outlawed from the beginning by the religious leaders and teachers of His day. Even Nathanael asked how anything good could come from Nazareth (John 1:46) and He was despised because of His lowly occupation as a carpenter (Mark 6:3). So bigoted were the Pharisees that not long after our Lord appeared on the scene, they sought to achieve His death. How do you think our Lord felt, being criticised and outlawed by those He came to save? Jesus knows how we feel when we too are subject to criticism and prejudice.

Opening our Eyes

If there is any doubt remaining in our minds about Jesus experiencing hurt when critical or insulting things were said about Him, then the text of 1 Peter 2:23 must settle the issue once and for all. Permit me to quote you the Amplified Bible translation: 'When He was reviled and insulted, He did not revile or offer insult in return; [when] He was abused and suffered, He made no threats [of vengeance]; but He trusted [Himself and everything] to Him Who judges fairly.' Did Jesus experience hurt when reviled and insulted? The text says so: 'when He was abused and suffered.' Because our Lord was human, He was affected by what people said about Him – He suffered – but He never allowed His hurt feelings to develop into bitterness or resentment. Why was Jesus so successful in allowing Himself to feel hurt but not allowing the hurt to develop into a root of bitterness? I think the answer is to be found in the phrase: 'He made no threats [of vengeance]; but He trusted Himself and everything to Him Who judges fairly.' When we get hurt, our natural (and sinful) reaction is to hurt the one who has hurt us. We cry out for justice – 'I have been hurt, now let the one who hurt me be hurt too.' That is the only perspective our carnal nature knows. Christ's attitude, however, was to transfer the whole matter into the hands of God and trust Himself and everything to Him who judges fairly. He handed responsibility for retaliation over to God: '"Vengeance is Mine, I will repay," says the Lord' (Rom. 12:19, NKJV). God's absolute justice heals wounded spirits.

Some would say that no one can ever hurt you by cruel or unkind criticism – you hurt yourself by responding to it incorrectly. One psychologist, Dr Albert Ellis, says:

> No one can ever hurt you by their criticisms of you. No matter how vicious or vituperative their criticism, the words they use do not have the power to produce within you the teensiest bit of discomfort. If you are hurt, the problem

arises because of the value and meaning you give to the words the person uses. Only one person has the power to put you down – you yourself. Cruel or unjust criticism hurts because it triggers off in your head ideas that are in harmony with the way you see yourself. If you didn't see yourself this way, the criticism would wash over you and fail to affect you.

Now there is a good deal of truth in this, of course, but it is not all the truth. Dr Ellis is widely known for his stoical approach to life – the approach that advocates developing indifference to both pleasure and pain. The Christian approach is to face and acknowledge your feelings and recognise they are there. It is not a sin to be hurt. This is a very human response to the instinct for self-preservation that is within all of us. It is a sin only when we harbour a hurt. In my opinion, cruel and unjust criticism would have hurt our Lord deeply, but He made sure that the hurt would be quickly offered to God and not allowed to develop into bitterness in His soul.

Consider the bigotry and prejudice of the Pharisees. One of the reasons why they were angry with Christ was because of His declared interest in 'others' such as 'sinners' and Gentiles. While it was true that the Jews were God's chosen people, our Lord made it equally clear that although He had come to them *first*, it was not to them *only*. The implications of His message were universal. Beginning at Jerusalem, it was to encompass the whole world. He had time for the Samaritan woman at the well; He had time for the Syro-Phoenician woman also. This greatly angered the Pharisees, for they saw in His actions an attempt to belittle the 'separated-ness' and spiritual superiority of their race. Christ was indifferent to their puritanism. The Pharisees would never have eaten with prostitutes, tax collectors and sinners – but Jesus did! (See Luke 7:36–39; 15:1–2.) When He identified with these 'outcasts', Christ suffered the same hurtful bigotry as them.

Discussion Starters

1. In what ways did Christ experience criticism and prejudice?

   _____
   _____
   _____
   _____
   _____

2. Why do mere words produce hurt in us?

   _____
   _____
   _____
   _____
   _____

3. How can we avoid criticism destroying us?

   _____
   _____
   _____
   _____
   _____

4. How can we ensure our criticism is helpful and constructive rather than destructive?

   _____
   _____
   _____
   _____
   _____

5. Why do people exhibit prejudice and criticise others destructively?

6. How do you feel about Christians of other denominations, and what fellowship do you have with them?

7. How should Christians relate to people of other faiths and ethnic origins?

8. When can pride in one's own group or nation become bigotry?

Final Thoughts

Jesus was subject to bigotry and was unjustly and unfairly criticised. When the tax collectors and sinners came to hear Jesus speak, the Pharisees and scribes complained that He received sinners and ate with them. Their criticism implied that because He associated with sinners and tax collectors, He was just like them – guilt by association. How did Jesus react to this? He would have been hurt by it, but the way He reacted to hurt was to turn everything over to God. In Luke 7 Jesus responded with the wonderful parable of the two debtors, and offered forgiveness to the repentant prostitute. A similar account in Luke 15 says 'Jesus told them this parable', and then He gave the parables of the lost sheep, the lost silver, and the lost son, all revelations of the seeking, redemptive God. What reactions to accusations – He turned them into revelations!

Take another occasion when the Pharisees watched Him to see whether He would heal a man with a withered hand on the Sabbath, so that they might criticise and condemn Him. The scripture says, 'He … looked around at them with anger, being grieved by the hardness of their hearts' (Mark 3:5, NKJV). In this action, our Lord defined the nature of righteous anger – grief at what is happening to another, rather than a grudge at what is happening to oneself. That reaction, too, was a revelation – a revelation of the nature of righteous anger. When next you are the subject of cruel and unjust criticism and the hurt penetrates deep into your soul, draw comfort from this fact: not only does Christ know how you feel, but He can help you make your reactions a revelation too.

Closing Prayer

Dear Lord Jesus, You overcame such immense criticism, hatred and bigotry by love, and by Your determination to live according to Your Father's will. You were never deflected from the truth. Lord, create in us hearts that respond to opposition in the same way, and lips that speak blessing to those who criticise and curse. Amen.

Physical Suffering and Pain

Icebreaker

How do you feel about the issue of suffering? Do you feel we should simply accept it stoically, or are you confused or angry as to why there is suffering in a world created by the God of love? How do you feel about Job's response of worshipping God when he heard that he had lost his possessions and all his children (Job 1:13–22)?

Opening Prayer

Dear Father, as we consider the issue of suffering and the death of Your Son, we pray that You will help us understand these things from Your perspective and not become confused by the inadequacy of human reasoning. In moments of perplexity, help us realise that the One who asks for our trust is the One who gave Himself for us on the cross. Amen.

Bible Readings

Mark 15:15–20

Wanting to satisfy the crowd, Pilate released Barabbas to them. He had Jesus flogged, and handed him over to be crucified.

The soldiers led Jesus away into the palace (that is, the Praetorium) and called together the whole company of soldiers. They put a purple robe on him, then twisted together a crown of thorns and set it on him. And they began to call out to him, 'Hail, king of the Jews!' Again and again they struck him on the head with a staff and spat on him. Falling on their knees, they paid homage to him. And when they had mocked him, they took off the purple robe and put his own clothes on him. Then they led him out to crucify him.

Hebrews 12:2–4 *(The Message)*

Keep your eyes on *Jesus*, who both began and finished this race we're in. Study how he did it. Because he never lost sight of where he was headed – that exhilarating finish in and with God – he could put up with anything along the way: cross, shame, whatever. And now he's *there*, in the place of honour, right alongside God. When you find yourselves flagging in your faith, go over that story again, item by item, that long litany of hostility he plowed through. *That* will shoot adrenaline into your souls!

In this all-out match against sin, others have suffered far worse than you, to say nothing of what Jesus went through – all that bloodshed! So don't feel sorry for yourselves.

Setting the Scene

We turn now to focus on another aspect of the way in which Christ has identified with our humanity – the aspect of suffering and pain. No one has suffered more than our Lord, and His experience in Gethsemane and on the cross are evidence of this fact. How do we begin to deal with this difficult problem of suffering and pain? It keeps raising its head, regardless of the most erudite attempts to explain it away. Even C.S. Lewis, who offered perhaps the most articulate explanation of it in modern times, saw his arguments wilt as he watched the onslaught of bone cancer in his wife's body. Sharing his feelings some time after the event, he wrote that you never know how much you believe anything till its truth or its falsehood become to you a matter of life and death. I know something of what he meant, having watched my wife die in a similar way. Like Hercules battling against the Hydra, all our attempts to chop down the arguments of the atheists and the agnostics in relation to suffering and pain are met

with writhing new examples, each one seemingly worse than the others.

Is suffering and pain, as some philosophers claim, God's big mistake? I do not believe so myself. I remember as a child having to have my tonsils removed and when the moment came to enter the hospital, I clung to my mother, pleading with her to save me from the ordeal. The look she gave me said, 'I must not save you from it. You will understand some day. You must trust my love.' This is how God deals with us in the presence of suffering and pain. He says, 'What I permit may not make much sense to you now … but there is a purpose. Trust My love!'

Opening our Eyes

Omnipotence, of course, could easily have avoided the problem of suffering, but only at the price of making us puppets on strings controlled by God. But by giving us free will, God had to take the risk that we would misuse and misapply our freedom. One writer uses the analogy of God making wood, a useful product, as the branches of a tree bear fruit and also support leaves that provide shade and shelter for birds, squirrels and other forms of wildlife. Even taken from the tree, wood is useful. People use it to build homes, to make furniture and many other useful things. Wood, however, is hard and therefore potentially dangerous. You can put a piece of wood in someone's hand and they can use it either to make something useful, or to break open the skull of another person. Of course, God could reach down each time one person hit another with a heavy piece of wood and turn the wood into a sponge so that it would bounce off lightly – but that is not what freedom is all about. Even with so-called natural disasters like earthquakes, much suffering is due to poor construction by corrupt builders intent on making greater profits, and an inadequate

response by the international community. Months after
C.S. Lewis's wife had died, a friend asked him while out
walking: if he were God, would he make a man like
a machine, or with the freedom to choose. C.S. Lewis
paused for a while and his sharp mind saw right through
to the core of the issue. If he were a machine, he would
not feel the intense pain he was going through at the
time, but then he realised he would not feel joy either.
His reply was short, but filled with deep understanding
– he would do as God did.

Let us consider the physical and mental sufferings of Christ
in Gethsemane when His sweat was as drops of blood.
One doctor says: 'Though rare, this is the phenomenon
of haematidrosis where, under great emotional stress, tiny
capillaries in the sweat glands break, mixing blood with
sweat. This process alone could have produced marked
weakness and shock.' After the arrest in the middle of
the night, Jesus was brought before the high priest, at
which point someone struck Him in the face. The palace
guards then blindfolded Him, and mockingly taunted Him
to identify them as they hit Him. In the early morning,
battered, bruised, dehydrated and exhausted from a
sleepless night, Jesus was taken across Jerusalem to the
Praetorium, where He was stripped naked and whipped.
Then a heavy beam was tied to His shoulders and for a
while He was forced to carry His cross until relieved of the
ordeal by Simon of Cyrene. At Golgotha, He was skewered
to that cross by iron nails and strung up like a dog to
die. If you still struggle over the mystery as to why God
allowed pain and suffering into His world, then I point you
to an even greater mystery – God has suffered too!

Some who wonder what I mean when I say, 'God's
wounds answer to our wounds', might find the story
of what happened to Joni Eareckson helpful and
enlightening[1]. During the summer of 1967 she was
instantly paralysed in a diving accident, and several

weeks later learnt that her condition would be permanent. As a quadriplegic, Joni's spirits fell to great depths and turning to her friend Jackie, she said, 'Help me die. Bring me some pills or a razor blade, even. I can't live inside a grotesque body like this.' Of course, Jackie couldn't bring herself to do what Joni asked, which served only to increase Joni's sense of helplessness. One night, as another friend, Cindy, sat reading with her, Cindy blurted out, 'Joni, Jesus knows how you feel – you aren't the only one – why, He was paralysed too.' Joni asked, 'What do you mean?' 'It's true,' said Cindy. 'Remember, He was nailed on a cross. His back was raw from beatings and He must have yearned for a way to move, to change positions or redistribute His weight. But He couldn't. He was paralysed by the nails.' The thought went deep into Joni's spirit. It had never occurred to her before that God had felt the exact piercing sensations that racked her body. 'At that moment,' said Joni, 'God came incredibly close.' This is always the effect upon those who realise that the God they serve knows exactly how they feel. May He come close, incredibly close, to you today.

Discussion Starters

1. What does suffering teach us about our world?

_____

_____

_____

2. What does suffering teach us about God?

_____

_____

_____

Physical Suffering and Pain

3. How have you coped with suffering?

_____

_____

_____

4. How do you personally reconcile a God of love with suffering?

_____

_____

_____

5. Why did Christ allow Himself to suffer so much?

_____

_____

_____

6. How does considering Christ's suffering help our own suffering?

_____

_____

_____

7. How may God use suffering for a greater good?

_____

_____

_____

8. How can faith help when understanding fails?

_____

_____

_____

Final Thoughts

How does Christ's suffering 2,000 years ago affect us now in the twenty-first century? One of the most moving stories I have ever read comes from the book *Ten Fingers for God* by Dorothy Clarke Wilson,[2] in which she tells the story of Dr Paul Brand who worked among leprosy patients in Velore, India. One evening Paul slipped in late to a patients' gathering, where the air was heavy with the stench of crowded bodies, stale spices and treated bandages. The patients implored him to speak to them and, reluctantly, because he had nothing prepared, he stood up in the midst of them. Pausing for a moment, he looked at their hands, some with no fingers, some with only a few stumps, and said, 'I am a hand surgeon, so when I meet people I can't help looking at their hands.' He went on to say that he would have liked to have had the chance to meet Christ and study His hands! He said, 'It hurts me to think of a nail being driven through His hands, for that would have made them appear horribly twisted and crippled.' As he said these words, the effect on the patients was electrifying. They looked at each other as if to say, 'Jesus was crippled like us; He, too, had clawed hands like ours.' Tears flowed down their cheeks. Suddenly they lifted their hands (or what was left of them) to heaven, as if with new pride and dignity. God's own response to suffering made theirs so much easier.

Those of you who are experiencing pain and suffering at this moment: reflect on the pierced hands of Jesus. The hardest part of suffering is the temptation to believe God is not with us in it – the idea that He reigns in some far-off splendour, untroubled by our woes. It is not true! Whenever we are in need of succour in our lives and Jesus comes alongside, the first thing that impresses itself into our consciousness is the fact that He has pierced hands. There is a kinship among those who suffer, which others cannot share. They understand each other! In moments of trial, our Lord has no need to say anything. It is enough that He shows us His hands.

Closing Prayer

O Lord Jesus, what a mystery – the God of the stars becomes the God of the scars. You do not just understand or feel for our pain, but You have actually felt our pain, and in an even greater measure. We pray that as we fix our eyes on You and remember Your suffering, we will not grow weary and lose heart, but instead be filled with wonder, love and praise that You would endure all that for us. Amen.

NOTES

1. Joni Eareckson Tada, *Joni* (London: Harper Collins).
2. Dorothy Clarke Wilson, *Ten Fingers for God* (London: Hodder Christian Paperbacks, 1985).

The Resurrection Power of Jesus

Icebreaker

What has impacted you most from our studies of the previous weeks? Try to share something about the sufferings of Jesus, and also something that has been particularly relevant to you personally.

Opening Prayer

Lord, we thank You that You willingly suffered for our sin so that we could be made righteous before God. It was through Your wounds that we could be healed. Hallelujah! We thank You for the resurrection and for Your Holy Spirit who now lives in us to transform us to be like Jesus. We thank You that when we experience suffering we can come before One who has experienced suffering, and so You can bind our wounds as no other. Amen.

Bible Readings

Isaiah 53:3–6

He was despised and rejected by men, a man of sorrows, and familiar with suffering. Like one from whom men hide their faces he was despised, and we esteemed him not. Surely he took up our infirmities and carried our sorrows, yet we considered him stricken by God, smitten by him, and afflicted. But he was pierced for our transgressions, he was crushed for our iniquities; the punishment that brought us peace was upon him, and by his wounds we are healed. We all, like sheep, have gone astray, each of us has turned to his own way; and the LORD has laid on him the iniquity of us all.

Romans 8:11,18

And if the Spirit of him who raised Jesus from the dead is living in you, he who raised Christ from the dead will also give life to your mortal bodies through his Spirit, who lives in you. ... I consider that our present sufferings are not worth comparing with the glory that will be revealed in us.

Hebrews 2:14–18; 4:14–16

Since the children have flesh and blood, he too shared in their humanity so that by his death he might destroy him who holds the power of death – that is, the devil – and free those who all their lives were held in slavery by their fear of death. For surely it is not angels he helps, but Abraham's descendants. For this reason he had to be made like his brothers in every way, in order that he might become a merciful and faithful high priest in service to God, and that he might make atonement for the sins of the people. Because he himself suffered when he was tempted, he is able to help those who are being tempted. ... Therefore, since we have a great high priest who has gone through the heavens, Jesus the Son of God, let us hold firmly to the faith we profess. For we do not have a high priest who is unable to sympathise with our weaknesses, but we have one who has been tempted in every way, just as we are – yet was without sin. Let us then approach the throne of grace with confidence, so that we may receive mercy and find grace to help us in our time of need.

Setting the Scene

Consider what our situation would be like if there were no resurrection. Elie Wiesel, who was a victim of the Holocaust, tells in his book *Night*[1] about an occasion in the concentration camp when he watched a child being hanged. He describes the child as having the face of a sad angel and as, along with others, he watched the brutal spectacle take place, he heard a voice behind him groan, 'Where is God? Where is He? Where can He be now?' Wiesel goes on to say that as a result of the things

he witnessed in the concentration camp, he became a pessimist. He writes: 'Can words like hope, happiness and joy ever have meaning again?'

I say, 'Yes, they can.' And here's why – Christ, too, went through a time when He cried, 'My God, my God, why have you forsaken me?' He knew what it was to identify fully with the pain and suffering which sometimes racks our bodies and our souls, but it didn't end there – it ended in resurrection. That's the hope the resurrection brings – the hope that sin, pain, suffering and death is not the end. Life is the end – glorious, everlasting, abundant life. The resurrection adds another layer to human experience and lets us know that whatever the reason God allows pain and suffering, they are beaten enemies. Difficult though it may be to believe, good will come out of them. The resurrection is the pledge that it will. Elie Wiesel came to the conclusion that God didn't care about His universe. As a result of suffering, many develop hard and bitter feelings towards the Almighty – as he did, or deny His existence altogether. How different from the story told by Corrie ten Boom in *The Hiding Place*. All the pain and suffering of *Night* are present in Corrie's gripping story of her own time in a concentration camp. Wiesel's book leads to unyielding despair, but Corrie's book leads to triumphant hope. What is the reason for this difference? It is the resurrection of our Lord. The resurrection is like a lighthouse in a storm-tossed sea of pain and suffering, beaming out a powerful message of life and hope. It says, 'Sin, pain and suffering are not the final answer – God is the final answer.' So have confidence in the confidence of God. His Son overcame everything life threw at Him, and He sits once again on the throne of the universe, having Himself endured the deepest agonies of human suffering. As Corrie ten Boom puts it in *The Hiding Place*: 'However deep the pit, God's love has gone deeper still.'[2]

Opening our Eyes

What practical effect does Christ's identification with our pain and suffering have upon those who go through dark and depressing experiences? Christian literature fairly bulges with the truth that those who have suffered, and suffered deeply, derived enormous strength from the fact that the God they served has also endured pain. In John 3:14–15 Jesus said, 'Just as Moses lifted up the snake in the desert, so the Son of Man must be lifted up, that everyone who believes in him may have eternal life.' This refers to an incident when those who suffered snake bites looked, in the obedience of faith in God's word, at a bronze snake on a pole and lived (Num. 21:8–9). Similarly we 'look' in faith to the crucified Christ and receive new life. We also saw in the last session that Hebrews 12:2–4 encourages us, when we experience suffering, to consider Christ's sufferings, for '*That* will shoot adrenaline into your souls!' The recognition that Christ suffered, inspires and comforts us in our own pain. Yet there is more. Paul exults that the resurrection was not only a powerful event in history, but was an explosive event in his life and experience also. It was more than a date on a calendar; it was a dynamic in his heart. He cries, 'I want to know Christ and the power of his resurrection …' (Phil. 3:10). Power normally comes from a throne, but Christ's power flows from a tomb. The power that was focused in bringing Christ back from the dead 2,000 years ago is available to you and me now – to save us, sanctify us, heal us, transform us and strengthen us.

There are many situations where God's power brings great deliverance from suffering. Yet even in the most faith-filled churches, honesty causes us to admit that people are lonely, hurting, and suffering in many ways. My own battle with prostate cancer for over ten years has brought me to moments of despondency. I do not pretend to be a warrior when it comes to illness, but I am aware that in the deepest and darkest moments there

is always a stream of strengthening and uplifting power that flows from God, and that this helps to comfort and sustain. People who are not Christians are puzzled by this power, which we commonly call 'grace'. They do not understand it at all. But my own experience has proved to me that what I have taught and believed, concerning the sustaining grace of God, is indeed a glorious fact. I have felt a resurrection power supporting me for which there can be no other explanation than that God is at work. When Paul asked God three times to take away the 'thorn in [his] flesh' he was promised, not deliverance, but grace to endure and use the infirmity (2 Cor. 12:8–10). When God does not take our suffering away, even though we continue to plead with Him, you can be sure He will give us a supply of grace that will enable us to cope with it. And not just cope but actually glory in our suffering, for '... Christ's power may rest on me. That is why, for Christ's sake, I delight in weaknesses, in insults, in hardships, in persecutions, in difficulties. For when I am weak, then I am strong.'

Christ's crucifixion and passion shows us a God who has experienced our wounds and can empathise *with* our suffering. Christ's resurrection power shows us a God who can minister His grace *to* our suffering. Either He will deliver us *from* it, or deliver us *in* it. But you have to be open to grace. When in need of grace, I come to God and picture myself standing under a waterfall, and open every cell of my body to Him. As soon as you open the doors of your being, I promise you, God's grace will flow in. How thankful I am that Christ's time on earth did not end in death and defeat, but in resurrection and victory. He is risen. Hallelujah!

Discussion Starters

1. Why did Jesus endure suffering? (See Heb.2:9–10; 5:9; 12:2)

2. How do we 'look' to Jesus?

3. What does the crucifixion mean for Christians?

4. What does the resurrection mean for Christians?

5. How can considering Christ's suffering *and* resurrection power help us when we suffer?

6. Can you define grace? How can we avail ourselves of God's grace?

_____

_____

_____

7. Why may we 'delight in our weaknesses'?

_____

_____

_____

8. What has impacted you most from this study?

_____

_____

_____

Final Thoughts

Christians are to follow in the steps of their Lord and turn their sufferings into good. The way in which this is to be done is beautifully illustrated by the experience of the oyster, into whose shell there comes one day a grain of sand. This tiny piece of sand lies there imposing pain and stress – so what shall the oyster do? Well, there are several possibilities. The oyster could, as so many men and women have done in times of adversity and trouble, openly rebel against God. The oyster, metaphorically speaking, could shake a fist in God's face and say, 'Why should this happen to me?' But it doesn't. Or it could say, 'It can't be true; this is not happening to me. I must not permit myself to believe it.' It doesn't do that, either. It could also say, 'There is no such thing as pain. It is an error of the mind. I must think positive thoughts.' But that is not what the oyster does. What, then, does it do?

Slowly and patiently, and with infinite care, the oyster builds upon the grain of sand layer upon layer of a white milky substance that covers every sharp corner and coats every cutting edge. And gradually … slowly … by and by, a pearl is made. The oyster has learned – by the will of God – to turn grains of sand into pearls. And that is the lesson we must learn along this pilgrim way. Surely it is something more than a metaphor when the Bible says that the entrance into the new Jerusalem is through a gate made of pearl. It is pointing out that the way into the city of God is through a wound that has been healed. Let God help you turn your pains into pearls, so that others can walk through them into joy and encouragement. I know some Christian counsellors whose approach to those who are hurting is to say, 'You are a Christian – you shouldn't feel like that.' I am glad that Christ does not deal with us on that basis. He says, 'I see you are hurt. I know what it is like, for I have been hurt too. Let me show you how to deal with it so that it does not infect your soul.' No wonder He is called the 'Wonderful Counsellor'.

Closing Prayer

Dear Lord Jesus, our hearts are overwhelmed when we consider how You allowed Yourself to suffer, for Your death has brought us life and Your wounds have healed our wounds. We thank You that Your grace and resurrection power still flows today so that when we are weak, You make us strong. We are eternally grateful. Help us not only to understand this message but also to live it and share it with others. Amen.

NOTES
1. Elie Wiesel, *Night* (London: Penguin, 1981).
2. Corrie ten Boom, *The Hiding Place* (London: Bantam Books, 1996).

Leader's Notes

Study One: Humiliation and Loneliness

Theologians refer to Philippians 2:5–8 as describing the *kenosis* experience of Jesus, from the original Greek of the New Testament translated in the NIV as 'made ... nothing' in Philippians 2:7. Strong's Greek dictionary defines *kenoo* as 'to make empty, i.e. (figuratively) to abase, neutralize, falsify, make (of none effect, of no reputation, void), be in vain.' The root Greek word *kenos* appears in Luke 20:10–11, where the servant of the vineyard's owner is sent away empty-handed by the tenants. In other words, he was given nothing. It has been said that when Christ left the glory of heaven and came to earth He emptied Himself of all but love and had nothing else. All the honour and privileges of divinity were forsaken in order that He might take on human flesh in a stinking filthy stable, and be laid as a helpless baby in a cattle-feeding trough. He truly became 'one of us'.

One of the things that concerns me deeply about much of modern-day Church life is the tendency of some leaders to practise denial. Let me remind you what denial is all about – it is looking at things as one would like them to be rather than as they really are. Can loneliness be completely resolved while we are here on earth, or merely relieved? My own view is that for some it may never be fully resolved, but only relieved. There are those whose loneliness is really of their own making because they have grown critical and self-pitying, and unconsciously drive folk away. Others find themselves unnecessarily lonely because of bitterness and unforgiveness. My concern, however, is for those who through no fault of their own find themselves in situations where they feel desperately lonely. The grace of Christ can flow in to ensure that the loneliness is not incapacitating or disabling, but it may be that one has to live with the sharpness of it until the day when faith is lost in sight. This, I know, runs counter to the teaching in many sections of the Church that says we can confidently expect complete spiritual satisfaction to be ours this side of heaven. The effect of this teaching is to assume that Christ's presence promises to take all the struggles out of the Christian life and give us heaven now. This is why our churches are full of Christians who pretend to feel now what they are not able to feel until they get to heaven – complete and total satisfaction. This is what they are taught, so whenever they struggle they say to themselves, 'Christians are not supposed to have struggles, so when someone asks me how I am, I had better not let the side down – so I will pretend things are fine.' Can you hear the denial going on in those words? Let me remind you that even though Adam walked in the Garden of Eden in perfect fellowship with God it was '... not good for the man to be alone ...' (Gen. 2:18). Those whose integrity will not allow them to pretend often worry that they are not making it spiritually, and think to themselves: 'Something must be wrong with my Christian life.' Churches tend to reward those who can create the illusion of having it all together by holding them up as examples of what a Christian should be – while actually, in some cases such people may be less spiritual than those whose integrity compels them not to deny their struggles.

Study Two: Temptation

What is the difference between a trial and a temptation? Take, for example, Job's trials. He lost his family, his home, his livestock, his health – everything. There was nothing immoral involved in those trials, although of course, in Job's case we have to recognise that they were not just natural disasters but were brought about by sinister intent. A clearer illustration of a trial might be that of John on the Isle of Patmos. He was banished to the island because of his commitment to Jesus Christ and was forced to live in isolation – removed from all those things that he would have held most dear. It was a trial. The same applies to Elijah who, in the midst of difficult circumstances, became depressed. When his life was threatened, he went away to hide and pleaded with God, 'It is enough! Now, LORD, take my life, for I am no better then my fathers' (1 Kings 19:4, NKJV). Temptation is different, for it has to do with more than circumstances – it contains a deliberate enticement to commit sin. It is not just experiencing an ordeal (though temptation can be an ordeal) but involves being solicited by evil to reject obedience to God in your life.

The issue of personal responsibility to avoid sin may cause debate, because some might question how weak human beings can overcome powerful forces of temptation. It may also conversely engender thoughts of self-righteousness and a form of salvation by self-effort. Both views are far from the truth. God's grace is available not just to save us after we have sinned but to save us from committing sin in the first place. Paul puts it this way in Romans 6:1–2: 'What shall we say, then? Shall we go on sinning, so that grace may increase? By no means! We died to sin; how can we live in it any longer?' He continues in chapters 6, 7 and 8 to reveal that just as we used to yield to 'impurity and … ever-increasing wickedness' so, through the Spirit of Christ, we should now yield our minds, bodies and spirits to righteousness. Other New Testament writers also emphasise this aspect of personal responsibility, when for example we are told by John to 'walk in the light' (1 John 1:5–10) and by Peter to 'abstain from sinful desires' (1 Pet. 2:11).

It is also important to note how Jesus overcame temptation in His own life. He did not argue or converse with the devil, but simply quoted an appropriate scripture and thereby allowed God to have the final say.

1 Corinthians 10:13 tells us, 'No temptation has seized you except what is common to man. And God is faithful; he will not let you be tempted beyond what you can bear. But when you are tempted, he will also provide a way out so that you can stand up under it.'

Study Three: Misunderstanding and Bereavement

Many Bible commentators believe that Psalm 140 was written by David as he was on the run and hunted by an angry King Saul. An explanation of this psalm brings out some principles which ought to help us next time we are misunderstood. The first thing to notice is that David recognised his predicament had been caused by exaggeration. When people misunderstand you, they exaggerate what you said or what you did and make it mean something you did not intend. Look how exaggeration affected David's enemies: 'They devise mischiefs in their heart; continually they gather together and stir up wars' (v.2, Amplified). Often misunderstanding starts with a slightly wrong interpretation and then gradually builds up to where a person is willing to believe out-and-out lies.

Next, David got in touch with his feelings and acknowledged his sense of vulnerability: 'Keep me, O LORD, from the hands of the wicked' (v.4). These are the words of a person who feels vulnerable and exposed. Vulnerability is one of the things that reverberate inside us whenever we are misunderstood. We are caught off our guard, we are not prepared or ready to deal with it, we feel trapped, naked, exposed. What do we do when this sort of thing happens? Look at the passage again: 'I said to the Lord, You are my God (v.6, Amplified). Notice, he *said* this to the Lord, not just thought it. Our dependence on God must be verbalised if it is to be realised. Talking to Him not only gets something out of us, it opens us up to God so that He might get something into us. We must, however, be careful to avoid *excessive* grief. Firstly, we should recognise that bereavement comes to us all and allow ourselves to feel the way God designed us to feel. If we bury grief it may ferment within us and poison our soul. We should surrender any bitterness or resentment into the hands of God, for it is this more than anything that is responsible for grief staying with us longer than it should. Finally, get alongside someone else who is grieving, and see what you can do for them. You are made tender by your sorrow, and that tenderness can make your service for Christ protective and effective.

Study Four: Criticism and Prejudice

There can be no doubt that bigotry and prejudice were abhorrent to Jesus Christ. He was hurt when He was on the receiving end of it, and He was hurt also when He observed others being subjected to it. On one occasion John turned to Him and said, 'Master, we saw someone casting out demons in Your name, and we forbade him because he does not follow with us' – and Jesus rebuked the Son of Thunder in no uncertain way (Luke 9:49–50, NKJV). It seems John made the announcement in the manner of a man who was rather pleased with his promptitude. Casting out demons! In Your name! Jesus soon sets the record straight and says, 'Do not forbid him, for he who is not against us is on our side.' The spirit of bigotry and prejudice did not die with apostolic times – it is with us still.

All down the ages, one group of Christ's disciples has been forbidding another group of Christ's disciples on no more serious grounds than 'they do not follow with us'. No one familiar with history and jealous for the honour of Jesus Christ can help feeling unutterably sad when they read the stories of how one section of Christ's

Church has persecuted another: the burning and torturing of Protestants in one generation, and the burning and torturing of Roman Catholics in another. Even different groups within the same denomination have opposed each other in a sectarian spirit. And all this undertaken in the name of Christ, who said, 'By this all will know that you are My disciples, if you have love for one another' (John 13:35, NKJV). Nor is it all ancient history. Even today, poisoned words are still flung about between one Christian group and another. Men and women wound each other in the tenderest part of their soul and think that in doing so, they are serving God. In bigotry and prejudice, there is almost always the disposition to persecute. Circumstances may prevent it finding any fiercer expression than through barbed or sarcastic words, but then words can sometimes wound more deeply than swords. The hateful heart of a bigot's sin is that they fail in love. People often ask me, 'What are we to do when others fail in love towards us, when they speak contemptuously of our particular viewpoint, when they deride our doctrines, when they say we are not really part of Christ's bride, when they pour scorn on our sincerity?' The answer is – we must go on loving. We must meet slander with affection, scorn with service, ostracism with the right hand of fellowship. We are followers of Him who said, 'He who is not against us is on our side.' If it is hard, then remember Jesus knows exactly how you feel. He, too, was the victim of bigotry and prejudice. Let His wounds heal your wounds.

Study Five: Physical Suffering and Pain

In the days prior to my conversion, one of the things that used to impress me about Christianity was its willingness to meet the issue of sin and suffering head on. Other religions set out to deny that pain existed, or encouraged their adherents to deal with it stoically. Many dodged the issue of pain – Christianity looked it squarely in the face. C.S. Lewis described suffering and pain as 'God's megaphone'. It is an appropriate phrase because it shouts to us that something is wrong. It was this aspect of Christianity that made G.K. Chesterton say, 'The modern philosopher told me I was in the right place but I still felt depressed, even in acquiescence. Then I heard that I was in the wrong place and my soul sang for joy.' What did he mean? The optimists of his day told him that this world was the best of all possible worlds and he should make the best of it. Christianity came along and told him that this is a stained, marred planet. This perspective then led him to say:

> It entirely reversed the reason for optimism. And the instant the reversal was made, it felt like the abrupt ease when a bone is put back in the socket. I had often called myself an optimist to avoid the too evident blasphemy of pessimism. But the optimism of the age was false and disheartening because it tried to prove we have to fit into the world.

Suffering and pain, God's megaphone, can either drive us from Him or draw us to Him. It can make us angry with God for allowing such conditions in His universe, or make us appreciative of God for building a new environment in which sin and sorrow will have no place (Rev. 21:1–5).

Suffering can also motivate us to demonstrate God's love in practical ways. Jesus healed the sick, released the oppressed, fed the hungry and loved the outcasts. Ultimately His suffering was eternally redemptive because it paid the penalty for our sin. His example inspired people like Wilberforce to abolish slavery, Fry to improve prisons, Shaftesbury to reform working conditions, Mother Teresa to care for the poor and Dunant to found the Red Cross (for which he was awarded the first Nobel Prize).

Study Six: The Resurrection Power of Jesus

There is a sense in which not only is our Lord a wounded Healer, but we are called to be wounded healers also. Just as our Lord's wounds give Him a special empathy for us in our struggles and sorrows, so our own wounds can be used to soothe and strengthen those who hurt. For example, it is a well-known fact in the field of counselling that the best helpers are those who have suffered the most hurts. Some time ago, I saw a videotape of Rollo May, a well-known counsellor in the United States, and I remember being deeply impressed with a statement he made which I cannot quote verbatim but which went something like this: 'Whenever I interview anyone who wants to join my team as a counsellor, the first thing I have to know is how much they have suffered. If they cannot convince me that they have experienced some suffering, then I tell them I have no use for them at the moment, and to come back when they have really suffered.' Strong words – but understandable. The more we have suffered, the more our sufferings can speak to others. And remember, you don't have to be a trained counsellor to help others. Every Christian has something to offer a brother or sister who is hurting if, as 2 Corinthians 1:3–7 points out, we let God comfort us and then pass on the same comfort to others. Shakespeare put it well when he said, 'He jests at scars that never felt a wound.'[1] Believe me, there is no more powerful ministry than to come alongside someone who is suffering, and share with them the fact that you have felt and received comfort for that selfsame hurt. Your weakness, under God, becomes someone else's strength.

1. *Romeo and Juliet*, Act II Scene II.

National Distributors

UK: (and countries not listed below)
CWR, Waverley Abbey House, Waverley Lane, Farnham, Surrey GU9 8EP.
Tel: (01252) 784700 Outside UK (+44) 1252 784700
AUSTRALIA: CMC Australasia, PO Box 519, Belmont, Victoria 3216.
Tel: (03) 5241 3288 Fax: (03) 5241 3290
CANADA: Cook Communications Ministries, PO Box 98, 55 Woodslee Avenue, Paris, Ontario N3L 3E5.
Tel: 1800 263 2664
GHANA: Challenge Enterprises of Ghana, PO Box 5723, Accra.
Tel: (021) 222437/223249 Fax: (021) 226227
HONG KONG: Cross Communications Ltd, 1/F, 562A Nathan Road, Kowloon.
Tel: 2780 1188 Fax: 2770 6229
INDIA: Crystal Communications, 10-3-18/4/1, East Marredpalli, Secunderabad – 500026, Andhra Pradesh.
Tel/Fax: (040) 27737145
KENYA: Keswick Books and Gifts Ltd, PO Box 10242, Nairobi.
Tel: (02) 331692/226047 Fax: (02) 728557
MALAYSIA: Salvation Book Centre (M) Sdn Bhd, 23 Jalan SS 2/64, 47300 Petaling Jaya, Selangor.
Tel: (03) 78766411/78766797 Fax: (03) 78757066/78756360
NEW ZEALAND: CMC Australasia, PO Box 36015, Lower Hutt.
Tel: 0800 449 408 Fax: 0800 449 049
NIGERIA: FBFM, Helen Baugh House, 96 St Finbarr's College Road, Akoka, Lagos.
Tel: (01) 7747429/4700218/825775/827264
PHILIPPINES: OMF Literature Inc, 776 Boni Avenue, Mandaluyong City.
Tel: (02) 531 2183 Fax: (02) 531 1960
SINGAPORE: Armour Publishing Pte Ltd, Block 203A Henderson Road,
11-06 Henderson Industrial Park, Singapore 159546.
Tel: 6 276 9976 Fax: 6 276 7564
SOUTH AFRICA: Struik Christian Books, 80 MacKenzie Street, PO Box 1144, Cape Town 8000.
Tel: (021) 462 4360 Fax: (021) 461 3612
SRI LANKA: Christombu Publications (Pvt) Ltd, Bartlett House, 65 Braybrooke Place, Colombo 2.
Tel: (9411) 2421073/2447665
TANZANIA: CLC Christian Book Centre, PO Box 1384, Mkwepu Street, Dar es Salaam.
Tel/Fax: (022) 2119439
USA: Cook Communications Ministries, PO Box 98, 55 Woodslee Avenue, Paris, Ontario N3L 3E5, Canada.
Tel: 1800 263 2664
ZIMBABWE: Word of Life Books (Pvt) Ltd, Christian Media Centre, 8 Aberdeen Road, Avondale,
PO Box A480 Avondale, Harare.
Tel: (04) 333355 or 091301188
For email addresses, visit the CWR website: www.cwr.org.uk
CWR is a registered charity – Number 294387
CWR is a limited company registered in England – Registration Number 1990308

Day and Residential Courses
Counselling Training
Leadership Development
Biblical Study Courses
Regional Seminars
Ministry to Women
Daily Devotionals
Books and Videos
Conference Centre

Trusted all Over the World

CWR HAS GAINED A WORLDWIDE reputation as a centre of excellence for Bible-based training and resources. From our headquarters at Waverley Abbey House, Farnham, England, we have been serving God's people for 40 years with a vision to help apply God's Word to everyday life and relationships. The daily devotional *Every Day with Jesus* is read by nearly a million readers an issue in more than 150 countries, and our unique courses in biblical studies and pastoral care are respected all over the world. Waverley Abbey House provides a conference centre in a tranquil setting.

For free brochures on our seminars and courses, conference facilities, or a catalogue of CWR resources, please contact us at the following address. **CWR, Waverley Abbey House, Waverley Lane, Farnham, Surrey GU9 8EP, UK**

Telephone: **+44 (0)1252 784700**
Email: **mail@cwr.org.uk**
Website: **www.cwr.org.uk**

 CWR Applying God's Word
to everyday life and relationships

Cover to Cover study guides
Genesis 1–11: Foundations of reality
Colossians: In Christ alone

Made up of seven sessions each, these helpful guides are ideal for group
and individual study. Jeremy Thomson looks at the early chapters
of Genesis and relates them to today's world: while John Houghton
examines the key book of Colossians, in which Paul writes of the
'adequacy, completeness and superiority of salvation in Christ alone'.

Genesis
ISBN-13: 978-1-85345-404-2
ISBN-10: 1-85345-404-4
£3.99

Colossians
ISBN-13: 978-1-85345-405-9
ISBN-10: 1-85345-405-2
£3.99

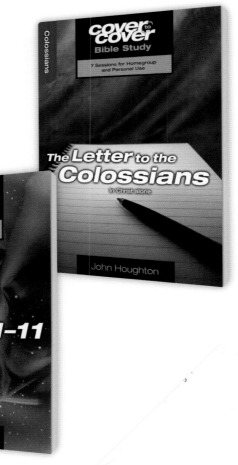

The Way of the Cross
Rob Frost

The aim of this Lent study guide, which can be used individually or
as part of a group, is to discover insights to help you to continue as an
effective follower of Jesus. It seeks to establish the 'way of the cross' as
integral to the life and spirituality of every contemporary Christian.

ISBN-13: 978-1-85345-353-3
ISBN-10: 1-85345-353-6
£5.99

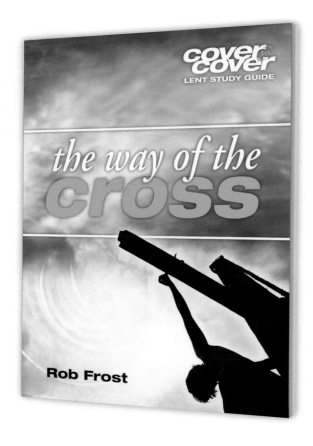

Immanuel - God with us
Anne Le Tissier

Are you looking for help in bringing spiritual focus to Christmas? If so, this 31-day inspirational guide through Advent, by respected writer Anne Le Tissier, will energise and inspire. Suitable for individual or group study.

ISBN-13: 978-1-85345-390-8
ISBN-10: 1-85345-390-0
£6.99

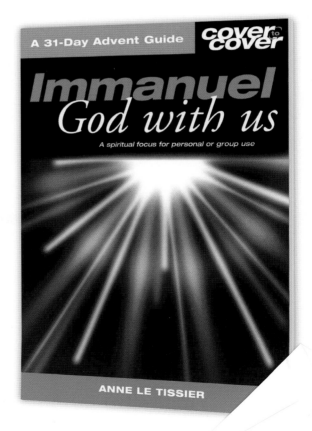